Colossians & Philemon

Live Transformed

Sarah K. Howley

Flaming Dove Press

Flaming Dove Press
an imprint of
InspiritEncourage LLC
1520 Belle View Blvd #5081
Alexandria, VA 22307
www.inspiritencourage.com

ISBN 978-1-960793-39-3 (e-pub)
ISBN 978-1-960793-40-9 (paperback)
ISBN 978-1-960793-41-6 (large print)

Printed in the United States of America

Library of Congress Control Number: 2025927129

Contents

Welcome

to this Study of Colossians & Philemon

Paul wrote the letter to the Colossians near the end of his life, around 60 AD, while imprisoned in Rome. Colossae was a city in Phrygia, or modern-day Turkey, and was an important trade center known for its textiles. The church in Colossae was planted by Epaphras, a believer from the church in Ephesus, and was composed of mostly Gentile believers. Paul indicated that he had not met the members of the church, suggesting he had not visited them.

During his imprisonment, Paul was visited by Epaphras and Onesimus. Their discussions must have prompted him to write both the Colossian church and Philemon, one of the members, to encourage and instruct them. This letter acknowledged and praised their faith and love, while also warning them about false teachings.

The letter to the Colossians presented Christ as the image of the invisible God and the source of reconciliation between God and humanity. It also addressed dangers of legalism and ends with practical guidance for daily conduct. Throughout the letter, Paul emphasized that believers' identity and maturity flowed from their position in Christ, with love as the basis for right living.

Paul's brief letter to Philemon was written around the same time as Colossians, possibly even carried by the same messenger. In Philemon, we see Paul's teaching on living a Christ-transformed life put into practice with faith expressing itself through love, forgiveness, and partnership in the gospel. You'll find a Bonus Session at the end of this study that explores this example of faith lived out in everyday relationships.

Though written to first believers in Asia, the message to the Colossians and to Philemon continue to challenge believers today to center their faith and practice on Christ alone. The letters invite reflection on what it means to live transformed lives - rooted in truth, growing in maturity, and grounded in love.

Each session opens with warm-up introductory questions, has a reading from Colossians and questions related to the passage. Then the study highlights the linked Old Testament passages and some reflection questions. Each study session ends with considerations for personal application. Additional tips and suggestions on approaching the study for individuals and groups follow.

Suggestions for this Study

This study is designed for individual or small group study and is composed of 7 sessions about Colossians and Philemon. It is designed to encourage thought and discussion of the scripture, inspiring individuals and groups seeking God to have conversations about the text. For 'You will seek me and find me when you seek me with all your heart,' as Jeremiah 29:13 says.

General Guidelines for Individual Study

1. Open each session with prayer. Ask God to speak through his Word.

2. Respond to the introductory questions that focus on the theme of the session and what God says in the main reading.

3. Read the passage more than once, perhaps in different translations. Using different translations can offer expanded viewpoints on the meaning of the original text. This study uses the New International Version (NIV) as the basis of questions

and quotes. However, any version may be used to provide insight and assist in revealing meaning.

4. This study is designed to offer a starting point for discovery of what God has to say to you through his Word. Because this study traces how the Old Testament is reflected in the epistles, it includes observation and interpretation questions on the Colossians and Philemon passage and on the Old Testament links, along with comparisons between them. Each session closes with application questions for personal reflection or group discussion. Writing your responses will provide clarity and focus your thoughts on the verses.

5. Use a Bible dictionary or other reference books to look up any unfamiliar words, places, or names.

General Guidelines for Group Study

1. Come to sessions prepared. Some groups will choose to read and respond ahead of time then gather and discuss together; others will gather to read and discuss together. Before beginning, agree how you would like to proceed so all are prepared.

2. Be an active participant in the group by sharing your thoughts and responses to the questions. Groups often have members who are in different places in their walk with Christ and each perspective should be valued.

3. Listen to each other. Consider the amount of time that is available for all to share and be careful not to dominate the conversation.

4. Be open-minded. Participants are encouraged to be open to learning and sharing, even expecting alternate viewpoints. The Bible serves as the foundation of this study and hearing other perspectives may challenge your own understanding. When differing views arise, the focus should remain on listening to each other and encouraging one another to wrestle with difficult passages and concepts rather than building consensus.

5. Maintain group confidentiality. For participants to be willing to share and grow, the trust level in the group must be high. Do not share what is shared in the group outside of the group unless permission is given to do so.

6. Expect God to meet you in the study. His Word is living and active (Heb. 4:12) and he is present when we gather in his name (Matt. 18:20).

Introduction

The epistles were written to early churches to help believers follow Jesus when the disciples were no longer present to guide them day to day. If you were writing a letter to believers today about living a transformed life in Christ, what guidance or encouragement would you include?

Paul's letter to the Colossians emphasizes transformation through Christ's love and presence. What would a transformed life look like to you?

Session 1: Faithful Believers

Colossians 1:1-14

Opening

Epaphras and the believers in Colossae are described as "faithful." How would you describe that term? What would the qualifications be for someone to be considered "faithful"?

What does a church look like when the congregants live in faith and love?

Paul's letter to the Colossians opened with gratitude to God for their faith, hope and love. He reminded them these gifts flow from God's grace and the Spirit at work within them. Paul encouraged believers to walk with the Holy Spirit, allowing him to shape their lives and to deepen their knowledge of Jesus. These words continue to call believers to walk faithfully with Christ in faith, hope and love today.

Read Colossians 1:1-14.

Reading Questions

Who made Paul an apostle?

How did Paul describe the Colossians?

What did Paul and Timothy thank God for as they prayed for the Colossians?

What did Paul ask God for in prayer for this church? Why did he ask for that? What effect would it have?

What kingdom did the Colossians belong to according to Paul?

What does redemption mean?

How have the believers been qualified to inherit? What is that inheritance?

Old Testament Links

The Christian's identity in Christ was a central theme in Paul's epistles. In this letter, strengthening the understanding of who believers are and the spiritual blessings they receive from God were key in walking with Christ. He drew on multiple images throughout the Old Testament to guide the Colossians in developing their identity in Christ.

Read Deuteronomy 7:6-9. How do these verses echo the opening from Paul to the Colossians?

2 Samuel 7:22-26 as well as the above passage in Deuteronomy mention redemption. Read this passage as well, and consider what image the Jews who read the letter would picture in relation to redemption.

Read Exodus 31:3; 35:31-32; Ezekiel 36:24-30, 39:29 and Joel 2:23-32. What blessings and promises were given to the people of God in these passages? How could those promises help understand the inheritance Paul described in Colossians 1:12?

Application

What insight does Paul's letter in verses 9-12 offer for us when we are praying for others?

The Colossians live in the Kingdom of Jesus, according to Paul. How do you understand your place in God's kingdom? What brought you into it, and what characterizes life there?

Session 2: Image of the Invisible God

Colossians 1:15-2:5

Opening

What titles or descriptor of Jesus come to mind when you think of him?

What does reconciliation to God mean?

Building on the focus on the Trinity in the first session, Paul turned to the supremacy of Christ while maintaining emphasis on his nearness to believers. With Christ dwelling in them, understanding Christ and growing to spiritual maturity becomes attainable. Paul urged the Colossians to remain united in love and confident of their knowledge of Christ because of this vital connection of Christ in them.

Read Colossians 1:15-2:5.

Reading Questions

In the original text, the description of Jesus in Colossians 1:15-20 is a poem or hymn. Note 3-5 of the titles given to Christ in this poem.

Verses 21-23 describe who believers were and who they become. Write the points Paul makes in the chart below.

Believers Were   Believers Became

In Colossians 1:25-27, Paul discussed characteristics of a faithful steward of the word. List them.

What was this mystery that Paul revealed?

What was the source of Paul's energy for ministry?

What goals did Paul have for the Colossians?

Old Testament Link

From the exalted position of Christ Jesus to the blessings his
followers receive, Paul encouraged the Colossians in this passage.
The Old Testament offers images and promises that point to
Christ's supremacy and to God's unfolding plan. As you read
the following passages, observe how they reveal Christ's role and
the mystery Paul described.

Genesis 1:27 says man was made in the image of God. What is
the difference between Colossians 1:15?

Read Proverbs 2:2-6. What echoes of this passage can be
found in Colossians 1:15-2:5? How does this repetition impact
conviction of those blessings received?

Application

Colossians 1:17 said, "... and in him all things hold together."
Share any experiences of Jesus "holding things together" in your

life? When have you felt them fall apart and how did that affect your dependence on God?

Paul said that the mystery revealed was Christ living in believers. What does it mean that Christ dwells in believers? In what ways does this truth feel easy to understand and in what ways is it still mysterious?

Session 3: Dependency on Christ

Colossians 2:6-23

Opening

According to the letter, the Colossians were being tempted away from walking with Christ and returned to their previous ways. What draws people away from Christian living these days?

When I return to my hometown, my accent often deepens the longer I am there. What other ways do we change based on the amount of time we spend with a group of people?

This session's reading focused on the need to stand firm in Christ and not be swayed by human traditions or rituals. It reminded the Colossians that Christ had freed them from dependence on rules and tradition so they could grow spiritually. The world of today likewise draws believers away from the centrality of Christ, and Paul's words continue to speak with relevance and clarity.

Read Colossians 2:6-23.

Reading Questions

How is a life "rooted and built up" in Christ, according to this passage?

What is emphasized about Christ in verses 9-10?

Paul describes the death and rising of believers in verses 11-15. How does that reasoning not allow for judgement referenced in verse 16?

Verses 8 and 20 mention "basic principles of this world." How do these fall short of life in Christ?

Much of this passage discusses false teachings and things that draw people away from Christ. List three things from the passage that draw people away from Christ.

Old Testament Links

The themes of circumcision, forgiveness, rootedness in Christ all echoed the promises given to Israel and fulfilled in Christ. The Old Testament revealed that the transformation of believers had always been part of God's plan. Life through renewal of the heart, freedom from sin, and growth through the personal presence of God were woven throughout the thread of Scripture.

Circumcision of the heart is key in Deuteronomy 30 as well as Colossians 2. Read Col. 2:9-15 and Deut. 30:1-10 and compare the requirements for "life" in the passages.

Read Isaiah 44:22 and Colossians 2:14. Isaiah described sins as already gone, centuries before Christ. How could Isaiah speak of forgiveness as already accomplished? How does Colossians 2:14 affirm Isaiah's statements?

Colossians 2:7 invokes agricultural imagery of being "rooted and built up." Consider Jeremiah 17:7-8 and Ezekiel 17:23 to outline the benefits of this rootedness.

Application

Verse seven speaks of teachings that strengthen faith. What teachings do you cling to when the Christian life gets hard?

Paul warns against being drawn away from Christ by the humanity that surrounds us. What are the strongest temptations for you to be drawn away or drawn into merely following rules?

Being holy or set apart is our calling as Christians, yet the world's rules or expectations can be difficult resist. Which worldly expectations do you find most challenging to oppose?

Session 4: Living Transformed

Colossians 3:1-17

Opening

What helps meaningful growth continue over time rather than remain a brief shift?

What kinds of things tend to capture people's attention or shape their priorities? How might a believer's focus or priorities differ?

Paul moved from describing the individual life in Christ to life in community and relationships with others in Chapter 3. This shift highlighted that believers live out the life of Christ within his body and among nonbelievers as well. They express his character in every relationship, private and public. This same call to reflect Christ's nature in community and in the world remains as relevant today as it was for the Colossian believers.

Read Colossians 3:1-17.

Reading Questions

What should a believer's mind and heart focus on?

What "earthly nature" did Paul characterize as idolatry? What reason did Paul give to "rid yourselves of all such things as these: anger, rage, malice, slander, and filthy language…"?

What difference did Paul describe between the old you and the new you in this passage?

Who are God's holy people and what virtues mark them (Colossians 3:11-17)?

What does the reign of peace look like since it "rules" in our hearts?

How does love bind in unity and Christ's peace rule? List three things that Paul mentioned.

Old Testament Links

Personal transformation through knowing God was a familiar theme for those well versed in Scripture during Paul's time. Emphasizing identity as God's chosen and beloved people, Paul recalled the promises delivered by prophets long ago. God's plan to renew the hearts of his people found fulfillment in Christ.

Colossians 3:12 describes God's people using the same language found in Deuteronomy 7:6-9. Why might Paul have chosen to repeat this description?

Colossians 3:5-14 echo the prophecies found in Ezekiel 11:18-20 and 36:25-27. How were these promises fulfilled in Christ?

Application

What do your mind and heart focus on most? How could you increase the percentage of thought toward the things above?

When considering Paul's lists in verse 5 and 8, which have been temptations to sin in your life? How has that temptation changed over time in Christ?

How does doing "whatever you do" in the name of Jesus change the attitude of the heart?

Session 5: Transformed Relationships

Colossians 3:18-4:1

Opening

What do you think helps relationships stay healthy and respectful, even when authority or responsibilities differ?

In today's culture, people often resist being told what to do. What helps someone respond well to guidance or authority?

Paul addressed family and work relationships in Ephesians and Galatians, as well as Colossians. These relationships form the foundation of daily life, involving the people with whom believers spend the most time. In the previous session, Paul reminded believers that they have put on a new self and now they need to live accordingly. He emphasized Christ is all and in all, Gentile and Jew, barbarian, Scythian, slave or free. This renewed identity was then to be expressed in everyday relationships, demonstrating God's transforming work in their lives.

Read Colossians 3:18-4:1.

Reading Questions

Paul offers a sort of pairing of relationships as he gives his instructions. First, outline what each half of the relationship's responsibilities are, then how they balance the responsibility of the other half.

Husband	Wife

How they balance:

Child   Parent

How they balance:

Worker   Master

How they balance:

Old Testament Links

From the beginning of Scripture, God set apart his people for relationship with Him and with one another. Though sin and pain entered the world and our daily lives, Old Testament figures were continually called to live in ways that reflected His character, and God encouraged such faithful living throughout His ongoing relationship with humanity.

What was the balance of responsibility between Adam and Eve before their fall compared to that of husband and wife according to these verses in Colossians? Consider Genesis 1:27-28, and 2:18, 21-24.

Proverbs 16:3 and Psalm 90:17 speak of work. How is its instruction similar or different from Colossians 3:23-24?

Application

Paul described relationships as a balance of freedom, responsibility, and sacrifice. How does that differ from how relationships are commonly viewed in society today?

The focus of the passage is relationships, which also require work to bind together in love and be ruled by peace (Colossians 3). How does this passage encourage you to live in the newness of life in family and work? Which of your relationships at home or work reflect the new self and which continue to carry parts of the old self?

Session 6: Mature and Fully Assured

Colossians 4:2-18

Opening

How can one have a consistent prayer life? What distracts from prayer?

When have words—spoken kindly or carelessly—had a lasting effect? What characterizes "wise" words?

Paul's closing to the church in Colossae shifts toward community life, persistent prayer and faithful partnership. This glimpse at Paul's connected and prayerful community encouraged believers to adopt similar practices and pursue unity.

These same patterns continue to mark mature followers of Christ today.

Read Colossians 4:2-18.

Reading Questions

What are at least three final teachings that Paul gives the Colossians in verses 2-6?

How do verses 7-18 demonstrate the importance of personal connection and love through others?

What was Epaphras' prayer for the Colossians?

Paul sent Tychicus and Onesimus to Colossae with this letter. He also encouraged the Colossians to read the letter to Laodicea. What does this say about gifts and teachings?

Why would Paul want people to remember his chains?

Old Testament Links

Paul's last words to the Colossians reflect patterns seen in God's people throughout the Old Testament. Faithful prayer, wise speech, gratitude, and partnership in service were longstanding themes of the Scriptures found among those who served God together in earlier generations. Paul's urgings to remain alert and dependent upon God were echoes of blessings and promises of His faithfulness.

Read Nehemiah 4:9 Psalm 5:3. How do these verses reflect Paul's call for alert, thankful prayer in Colossians 4:2?

Read Proverbs 15:1-2 and 16:24. What do these verses reveal about speech? How do they relate to Paul's teaching in Colossians 4:6?

Application

Would you describe yourself as consistent in prayer? What practices might help you grow in making prayer more continual?

Paul's list of companions and greetings in this passage reflects partnerships seen throughout Scripture (David and his mighty men, Nehemiah and his builders, Moses and Aaron). Who are your companions or partners in faith, and how might you strengthen that relationship?

Session 7: Faith's Transforming Power

Philemon 1-25

Opening

Forgiveness can feel costly. What do you think makes it so challenging for people to extend grace?

What helps people choose what's right when it's uncomfortable or unpopular?

Paul wrote to Philemon regarding an offense in work and church life. The letter is a demonstration of how lives are transformed by Christ and how to live them out in community. Paul's appeal to Philemon showed how faith in Christ redefines human relationships with love, grace, and partnership in the Lord.

Read Philemon 1-25.

Reading Questions

What did Paul thank God for about the letter recipients?

What did Paul pray for them?

How did Paul characterize his relationship with Onesimus?

Describe the relationship between Paul and Philemon according to the passage.

What was Onesimus' relationship to Philemon and how did it change?

What was Paul's request of Philemon and how was it framed?

Old Testament Links

Paul's appeal to Philemon aligned with long-standing themes of mercy, redemption, and justice found throughout the Scriptures. From laws protecting servants to stories of forgiveness and redemption, the Bible consistently revealed God's heart for restoration. These illustrations of God's people being called to act with compassion and seek restoration find their fullest expression in Christ.

In Deuteronomy 15:12-15, God described appropriate treatment of slaves. Summarize the characteristics revealed in the passage. How are those characteristics presented in Philemon?

Paul took on the role of intercessor for Onesimus in writing this epistle. Both Moses and Abraham interceded in the Old Testament. How do Genesis 18:22-33 and Exodus 32:11-14 demonstrates God's priorities in judgement and restoration?

Application

Philemon's faith was known to refresh others. What habits or attitudes could you cultivate to bring similar encouragement to others?

Paul described Onesimus as "no longer a slave, but better than a slave—a dear brother." How might faith in Christ reshape the way you treat those who depend on you or those whose decisions you struggle to accept?

Conclusion

Paul's letter to the Colossians revealed how the supremacy of Christ changes every part of life. Through him, believers were called to live transformed as new creations - renewed in mind and heart while growing in gratitude, unity, and love. This transformation touched daily life, shaping relationships, work, and community so that Christ dwelled both in and among them. The brief epistle to Philemon offered a glimpse of this transformation in practice, demonstrating how the gospel restores relationships and invites believers to extend grace as they have received it. Together, the two letters proclaimed that Christ is not only above all but present and active within believers, making His life visible within theirs.

How has the book of Colossians challenged the way you think about daily life (work, family, community) as expressions of faith in Christ?

Philemon highlights reconciliation, humility, and seeing one another through the lens of Christ. Which of these themes most shapes the way you understand your own relationships today?

In what areas of your attitude, priorities, or relationships do you sense Christ inviting transformation?

What did you learn about God from this study?

What did you learn about yourself from this study?

Do you believe that Jesus is the Messiah, the Son of God and have you received life in his name? If so, describe the qualities of that life.

If this is the first time that you have answered yes to the call of following Jesus, please reach out to a local church or the author to share of your choice and find support for your new life.

To continue your deep dive into "Seeing the Old Testament in the Epistles", pick up *1,2&3 John: Dwell in Light* to continue your study. Find it at your nearest retailer by scanning the QR code today.

1,2&3 John: Dwell in Light

Also By Sarah K. Howley

Seeing the Old Testament in the Epistles

Ephesians: Experience God's Power

James: Know God's Wisdom

1&2 Thessalonians: Prepare for Christ's Return

Hebrews: Elevate Jesus

Philippians: Pursue Christ's Joy

1&2 Peter: Grow in Grace

Revelation: Worship the Lamb

Colossians & Philemon: Live Transformed

1,2&3 John: Dwell in Light

Romans: Trust God's Gospel

The Son Reveals the Father

I Am: An 8-Session Study of John

Heart: A 12-Session Study of Luke

Word: An 11-Session Study of Matthew

King: An 8-Session Study of Mark

Our Trustworthy God: How Much God loves You, Joyfully

Engages with You, and Trusts You

Women of the Old Testament Bible Studies
Hope: A Bible Study of Women in Jesus' Lineage
Faith (coming 2026)
Love (coming 2026)

Alive Again Bible Study on Forgiveness
Alive Again: Find Healing in in Forgiveness
Alive Again Bible Study: Find Healing in Forgiveness
Alive Again Forgiveness Prayer Journal

About the Author

Author and founder of InspiritEncourage, Sarah K. Howley writes Bible studies that reveal the transforming depth of Scripture and lead readers into a thriving relationship with God. Known for weaving Old and New Testament connections with warmth and insight, she invites believers to encounter God's truth in everyday life. She fuels her writing with espresso—and gratitude for any gluten-free/dairy-free dessert she didn't bake herself. Sarah and her husband support global initiatives for literacy and hunger relief.

You can find Sarah on Facebook and Instagram @inspiritencourage. To book Sarah as a speaker at your next event, please contact her through her website. For weekly encouragement and information on her latest releases, sign up for Sarah's newsletter at InspiritEncourage.com.

InspiritEncourage